SPIRITUALIZING EVERYDAY LIFE

AND

WORSHIP OF THE SPIRIT BY THE SPIRIT

SWAMI ASHOKANANDA

Vedanta Society of Northern California

Originally published in the present form by
The Vedanta Society of Northern California in 1987
2323 Vallejo Street
San Francisco, California 94123

ISBN 0-9612388-0-1

The lectures *Spiritualizing Everyday Life* and *Worship of the Spirit by the Spirit* were delivered and recorded on the Sunday mornings of, respectively, November 24, 1957, and January 30, 1955, at the Vedanta Society of Northern California, Old Temple, San Francisco. Both lectures were previously published as separate booklets and have been slightly re-edited for the present edition.

SPIRITUALIZING EVERYDAY LIFE

SPIRITUALIZING EVERYDAY LIFE

1

LAST Sunday I spoke on the subject of worship—what it is and how to perform it. In connection with that subject, I said very briefly that if one is not inclined to perform worship of God in a ceremonial way there is another kind of worship and that is the worship of God in man. It is my intention to speak on that kind of worship this morning, and in this connection I think I should make, not exactly a confession, but a few prefatory remarks.

I am not trying to say that the practice of ritualistic worship is not necessary. Some such practice probably is universally needed. But I want to say that this is not the only kind of worship. There is another kind which I myself prefer. Of course, I like all forms of spiritual practice, all forms of worship; I have not found any conflict amongst them, but I think one is permitted to have a greater liking for one kind than for another; and the worship of God in man is a ritual, if I may call it so, closer to my heart than any other kind of ritualistic practice. You see, first of all, I am somewhat of an intellectual by nature and then I try to be philosophical, and I have found that this kind of practice follows naturally from the highest type of philosophy in Vedanta.

Swami Vivekananda used to call the application of Vedanta in its highest form "practical Vedanta." I sometimes think that this teaching, if it was not the central, was next to the central teaching of Swami Vivekananda. I regard his central teaching to be the divinity of man. Man, he said, is by nature perfect, infinite, and eternal, now and always. He wanted every person to become aware of his own spiritual, divine nature; he thought that was the most important thing for man in the present age, in the West as well as in the East. Next in importance was, I think, his teaching of the worship of God in man.

You see, it naturally follows that if I regard my own nature as divine I must also regard your nature as divine. I could not say that I am divine and you are just human or animal; that would be a contradiction in logic. Everybody is divine, and if we have this feeling in our present state where we still have a sense of outward relationship, our attitude towards other beings will be one of worship. Of course, when you become plunged in the consciousness of at-onement with God then you do not know that there is either an inside or an outside. In that very high, inarticulate state in which there is no thought, no movement, nothing, there is no sense of plurality, and the practice of regarding others as divine would not apply. But as long as you are aware of even one other person existing besides yourself—and in our ordinary state we are aware of an infinite number of beings existing outside of us—then, with the philosophical conviction in the background that everyone is indeed divine, the only true attitude you can maintain towards others is that of worshipfulness.

And if you are really conscious of the existence of divinity in another person you will find your whole being wants to bow down in reverence before that person. Whether you are yourself God or not is not the point. There is a subtle psychological fact to be taken into consideration: If I regard you as God, if I look at you and become conscious that you are divine, that you are no ordinary man but are God Himself—if I have that consciousness, I will not be aware of myself, I will be aware of you alone. That is the point to notice. And who, being aware of the presence of divinity before him, could remain unmoved? Who could fail to feel a profound sense of reverence and worship? And it is this sense of reverence that will actuate you to make self-sacrifice, to render homage to others, to do whatever you can for them.

2

Before I go further with the discussion, I think I should clear up one or two points. It naturally follows from the highest philosophical consideration of what constitutes the real, that God alone is real, and nothing else. It will not do, if you become thoughtful, to say that God created everything but shines in His own glory isolated and separated from all other beings. It seems so easy to say, "God created the world, God created men, God created angels, God created animals, God created this and that, and He created it all for the delectation of human beings." Such a view, to be sure, is very satisfying to a childish mind. As long as the brain has not developed and has not learned to think, this kind of statement is wonderful.

Some who are a little more thoughtful say, "These things are His glory, manifestations of His power." This is a very fine thought, but if these are manifestations of His power, what are they in themselves? Are they like pieces of furniture that are the manifestation of the carpenter? Furniture is made of wood though the carpenter himself is a conscious being. Is it that kind of manifestation? Or is it a transformation of part of the Lord's own being? Many have thought of it in the latter way. Sometimes they have said, "It is a manifestation in the same way as light is the manifestation of the sun." Basically the sun and the sunlight are identical, and yet there is, rightly I think, a distinction between the two. Some have said this whole universe is His glory in that sense. Yet here, too, you come to difficulties. If God and His universe are basically the same, then matter must be the same as God, although to our ordinary view they might appear as different.

So you find yourself coming to the position of Advaita or monistic Vedanta as the only tenable position: there is only one reality and that is the divine reality. You might ask—indeed you naturally would and should ask—how, then, does one explain this world of matter and of life, which is so very different in character from the divine reality, so imperfect, so (one might almost say) opposite to the divine nature?

The Vedantists of this school have put forward a wonderful explanation. It sounds at first simply clever, and you know how people are leery of clever answers; for however clever an answer is, there is a suspicion it may not be true. However, I don't call the monist answer just clever, because I know it is true. It is this: All this diversity, this appearance of the manifold, is like a dream experience, like a hallucination; as such it does not affect the true divine nature of reality. There is the classical illustration given by these philosophers: if you mistake a rope for a snake in the dusk, it does not mean that the rope actually has become a snake. Rather, there has been a superimposition of the illusion of a snake on the actual rope. The rope is a rope all the time. If you ask, "But how did this illusion come about originally? If there is only one reality, how could there be an illusion of manifoldness?" then they answer, "In ignorance there is no consistency." How *do* we mistake one thing for another? Do we do it rationally? If it were rational, then we would not have made any mistake. That we have made a mistake means that it is an irrational, an inexplicable something. If you then say, as some have, "The illusion always exists as opposed to pure divinity," then you are forced to accept the position of a dualist, though of a different kind, it is true. The answer is simply this—when you find the truth, ignorance vanishes. Then you do not say ignorance is one reality and truth is another reality; you never think that. Ignorance is ignorance, and you never put it under the same category as truth or the real. But these philosophers point out to us that the problem of illusion is coexistent with our state of ignorance. These arguments—that there is plurality and that it is to be explained this way or that way, that it is dreamlike or not dreamlike—all these arguments and problems exist *only* when we are ignorant. When we are illumined, they vanish away; indeed even the memory of the problems and of the answers vanishes away. All these things become nonexistent totally. And if such is the case, then, although it is a mysterious thing, this ignorance, in our present state we are not seriously handicapped so far as our ultimate knowledge of reality or truth is concerned.

This kind of reasoning, in which I, at least, have not found any loophole, forces me, as I think it should force everybody, to the conclusion that everything that is, is divine. Therefore if I am to be true—and we all want to be true, none of us want to be false for a single moment—I must learn to see everything as it really is, that is to say, as divine. You cannot get away from that position. This kind of philosophical impetus forces you to the practice of spiritualizing everything that you know, everything that you do. It forces you to do that. There is no escape from it.

A second thing one might say, "Well, I am not interested in this kind of spiritualization. Yes, everything is divine and someday I shall realize everything as divine. In the meantime I would like to just worship God; whether He is the creator or not, whether he is one with the creation or separate from creation, God is God nevertheless, and I am content to worship him as such." Yes, that is a legitimate position, but I think a time comes when you have to face the issue, when you are compelled to spiritualize everything.

You know, the world doesn't just exist, it exists related to our own self-interest. Why do you think the world exists? You will say, "Well, the world is there as an objective reality. What am I to do about it? It exists. Just as you are standing on the platform and I have to acknowledge your presence there, in the same way, the world is there." No, that is not true. Even if you were to assume the position that the world was created independently of you, still your perception of the world, your experience of the world, depends upon the state of your own mind. And I shall put forward the extreme position maintained by our philosophers in this respect. They have held that if you lose your interest in this world completely, then this world, whether projected by yourself or made by God, will totally disappear; you will not even be able to perceive it. This sounds a bit extreme, and some of you might be tempted to think, "That is just one of those theories; one cannot take such things very seriously." Of course, as long as you do not take the spiritual quest seriously or do not want to embrace the truth fully, then to you these things *are* just theories. When we cannot or do not want to do something, to us it is just a theory, and we say, "It does not apply to me. Let others think about it; I don't have to bother about it." But I say a time will come for every one of you when you will have to take these things seriously. You cannot realize God, who is infinite, unless you yourself have given your whole being to God. In that dedication of your whole being, you yourself will become infinite; and in that infinitude you will become aware of the infinite presence of God. This is a psychological fact, if I may use that term, although the mind in that state is so refined and so calm that "psychological" in the ordinary sense cannot be applied there. Let us say instead that it is epistemologically a necessity: when you yourself have become infinite, you will comprehend the infinite. And you become infinite when you have given your all to God, dedicated your all to God. In such dedication you become released from the bondages of the finite. The compulsion to see other things than God, it is this that makes us finite.

If your mind ever becomes quiet, appreciably quiet, then, even with the very best senses present and fully functioning, it will seem to you as if someone is erasing this universe. It is as though there were beautifully and clearly written letters on a blackboard and someone were erasing them; they slowly become blurred, their forms slowly disappear. You may say, "Yes, we experience that when we feel sleepy. When we get drowsy then things begin to disappear." It is something like that, but whereas drowsiness comes in spite of yourself, in that spiritual drowsiness the mind becomes concentrated on God, and a kind of release from the senses comes; the senses and the mind become inactive, drowsy, but your consciousness becomes exceedingly heightened. Thus this drowsiness has been called in Sanskrit *yoga-nidrā,* the "sleep of yoga". Yes, the body is asleep; the body has become quiescent, the mind has become quiescent; but the soul is awake to the consciousness of God. "Drowsiness" is an apt illustration of that state. I am not speaking of *samādhi* or any such thing; you are still functioning in your senses and are quite wide awake, yet everything seems shadowlike. If you were honestly to report your experience of the world at that time you would say, "All these things are just shadows." Swami Vivekananda once wrote in a letter, "Everything in the universe appears to me now like pictures hanging on the wall of a room."[1] A person who has attained to that state finds that the whole universe has become a two-dimensional affair; there is no concrete reality, just shadows. And even these after a time become obliterated.

It doesn't matter what your religion is or what kind of practices you follow, when your soul has become absorbed in God, wholly or to a very great extent, you are bound to come to the realization that only God is, nothing else is. Then, when you are faced with this world you have to relate it to God. Various religions prescribe various ways of doing this. Some say, "We should respect the creatures of God, take care of them and be kind to them"; others, "They are all children of God and therefore I should be respectful to them and serve them"; or, if the religion is more philosophical, "They are of the very being of God."

There comes another compulsion which I think many feel. It is this: You find that the total reality must be contained in your understanding of God, in your comprehension of Him. You do not want to say, "I shall be satisfied with God and leave the world behind." You feel that to do so would mean giving up part of reality, that your quest for truth would not be a total quest. When this uncomfortable mental situation comes, you are forced to go back to the world, you are forced to try to find what this reality is which we call the world and what these beings are that we call men. There, also, comes the necessity for spiritualizing everything.

3

Probably it is unnecessary for me to elaborate the point further that spiritual growth is a quest for unity; and as we grow more and more spiritual, our inner being becomes more and more unified: we do not want to do anything except serve God; we want only to think about Him, to love Him; we do not want to do anything else. And yet there are other things we must do.

Suppose there is a householder. He has a wife and children, he has other relatives; he loves them all and has duties towards them. What is he going to do? Is he going to say, "I shall do my duty, but when that is done I shall just ignore them and think about God"? Yes, that is one attitude, but another attitude is to spiritualize your relation with other beings, to see your relatives with other eyes than before. One of the ways very common in India is to say that God Himself has taken the form of your relative. A Hindu husband, for example, will look upon his wife as the embodiment of Shakti, the Divine Mother or Divine Power; so a person in speaking of somebody's wife will refer to her as his Shakti. The women of the family, whether wife, daughter, or sister, all have names of the Divine Mother, and the men—husband, son, or brother—have names of God. Names of God are given to the children, so when you call them by name you have the benefit of remembering the Lord. This custom has become a part of Indian life. A Vaishnava family will give their children Vaishnava names; a Shakta family, Shakta names; and a monistic-Vedanta family, monistic-Vedanta names. There came here during the 1939 International Exposition a Hindu family from northern India. The lady was very venturesome and had a shop at the fairground. While here she gave birth to a child and sent a request to me that I come and name it. The family was of monistic persuasion, and she was very particular that I give her child a monistic-Vedanta name; she would not stand for any dualistic name, so I selected the name Ātmaprakāsha, which is a highly philosophical name, meaning Self-luminous. That is the way Indian parents name their children, and they try to treat them accordingly.

It is not easy. You look upon a child as God and at the same time you have to thrash him when he becomes naughty; it is not easy. It requires a great deal of cleverness; you must inwardly say, "Lord, You have come to me as a child and therefore when

I take the cane and give You a hiding that is my worship, O Lord, so don't take it amiss." Or if you go to a sick person, you recognize that the sick person is God, but you do not prepare all kinds of sweets and such things to offer him; you bring him "sick diet," maybe sometimes you scold him, or hold him down in the bed if he tries to get up. All these things can be done in a worshipful spirit. I do not really see any difficulty about it; it is all in the attitude of mind you have. If you say that it is not possible to have proper reverence while you are engaged in disciplinary action, I shall give my own testimony in this regard. I have practiced this and I have found that it works. You may discipline a person and be very hard on him when it is a necessity of your service to him—not because of any emotion or impulse on your own part, not because you have become annoyed or irritated, but because you think it is the attitude that will accomplish what you want to accomplish for that person. Inwardly you think, "Lord, this is an offering to You. An offering on my part to You." You can be as hard as the occasion requires, and yet at the same time you can maintain the attitude of worship, and it is wonderfully effective.

It is effective in various ways. It actually gives you the sense of having been in a profound meditation. You may be working, you may be talking, but after you have finished, because of this inner attitude you feel as if you have come out of meditation. Moreover, it is often difficult to meditate on the absent God, the God made up out of your own mind. You may sit before a picture, or before a symbol such as the cross, but it may be very hard to imagine the presence of God there; you try, of course, and sometimes you feel it and other times you don't. But when you are in the presence of a living being and have persuaded yourself that this living being—the person that is looking through these eyes, moving these hands and these feet, uttering this speech, eating this food—that this real being is God Himself, then indeed you stand in the presence of the living God. It is not imagination. When first you begin to catch a glimse of this fact you are shaken through and through, for it is not easy to stand in the presence of the living God. We are doing it anyhow, but we have persuaded ourselves that all people are just ordinary. We look at one person and say, "Oh, he is a fool." at another and say, "Oh, he is a goody-goody," at another and say, "He looks awfully clever," or "Here is a real man." We make all these distinctions and differences; not for a moment do we think we are standing in the presence of God. But in this practice you are forced to recognize it. Nor is it just thinking; your whole being participates in it. It is very nice to gather a few flowers, very nice to burn a little incense and light a little candle—a few minutes and it is finished. There is no trouble about it. But go and nurse a sick man. He is troublesome, and his condition may become precarious; then you are upset about it. You cannot just let yourself go. Sometimes people worshiping or meditating fall asleep. The Lord does not come and whack them on the head as the Zen teachers do. The Lord remains silent; what He thinks He does not tell you. But you could not fall asleep with a sick man; you have to be alert. Unless you are a brute you will not allow anything to happen to your patient; you will be all the time alert. You will give him his medicine at the right time and his diet at the right time. You will attend to his comfort in every way possible. Your mind, your body, your emotions, everything has to be there; a great concentration is required; and mind that, all this time you have to maintain the consciousness that he is God Himself in the form of a sick man. All this calls for faculties not activated by ordinary worship.

I admit this is a difficult practice—any practice that becomes effective is difficult in the beginning—but if you just undertake simple practices which you are already able to do and let it go at that, you will not get very far. Yes, a time comes for every one of us when we have to take the bull by the horns. Spiritual growth is a challenge. It is not just floating down the stream merrily, it is swimming against the current. The time comes when you will recognize that there are certain propensities, thoughts, and emotions in you which are not in conformity with the truth but inimical to it and continually hampering your growth. You will be forced to remove these obstructions from your spiritual path. Then, of course, this practice becomes difficult, for whatever your path is, whether the path of devotion, of mental concentration, or of reasoning, or a mixture of these, when the time comes for you to take it seriously, it will invariably appear difficult until it has been mastered. Any practice, I repeat, will appear difficult if it is to be productive of results. But the beauty about this particular practice is that once you overcome the initial difficulties, which I admit are considerable, it becomes extraordinarily fruitful.

4

What are the initial difficulties? Let me point them out again. First of all, you must have a philosopy behind this whole practice, and the most apposite philosophy would be the philosophy of monistic Vedanta, which maintains that God alone is, that nothing else is, and that to perceive the real as divine is in accord with the truth.

It must have occurred to you that it is strange indeed, if everything is really God, that we do not perceive *anything* as God. We do not even perceive God, much less perceive everything as God. On the contrary, we perceive everything as material, or at best as living matter. We may call some living beings conscious, but we do not even know what we mean by "conscious." So, if you arrive at a point where you believe that the universe is pervaded by the divine presence, you must ask yourself why it is you do not perceive this presence.

I once asked myself that question. It seemed so strange to be thinking everything is other than God, while everything is really God Himself that I made some effort to think in accord with the truth, and I found that it brought results. I won't go so far as to say that I began to see God everywhere; but I will say that if we take a determined stand, this illusion of a material universe has a way of becoming obliterated. It requires a change of vision, a change of attitude. Again and again our mind will go back to the old way of looking at things, we shall forget that a man is really not a man but God Himself; then we have to bring our mind back to the right attitude. It is of course a tremendous struggle. But if your philosophy has been well founded, if, in your heart of hearts, you have been convinced that God alone is, nothing else is, you will find that eventually the difficulty goes away.

Secondly, it is not enough simply to assert this philosophy and to say, "I shall think the right thought, everything is divine, everything is God." You have to correct all the attendant and associated thoughts; you have to live by this philosophy in thought, in feeling, in action. You have learned to love and to hate: you select somebody and say, "I like this person," and you select somebody else and say, "I don't like that person." You get hurt if somebody does something to you, or doesn't do something to you. What is it that gets hurt? Who is it who has done things to you? It certainly is not your Self that gets hurt; it is incapable of getting hurt. And the person who has done hurtful things to you is really no one but God. Then against whom are you complaining? You are finding fault with God Himself! Such contradictions you will find so deadly that you will be forced to remove them from within yourself. Slowly and slowly you remove them. You learn to be infinitely patient. You feel that it is the ego that gets annoyed or irritated or hurt, that actually everything that comes, comes from God and cannot therefore be wrong; it cannot therefore hurt you. Then, all this selecting—"I like this person; I do not like that person"—you feel that it all comes from the ego; the ego wants to satisfy itself in various ways. We find that although we think we love people and are living just for them, actually we are not. It is a terrible thing to say, but our primal motive is self-interest.

In the *Bṛhadāraṇyaka Upaniṣad* there is a discourse given by a husband who was an illumined soul to his wife, in which he said, "O Maitreyi, it is not for the sake of the husband that the husband is dear to the wife, but for the sake of oneself that the husband is dear to the wife."[2] This is a disputed passage and has been variously translated. Swami Vivekananda used to give a different translation: "It is not for the sake of the husband that the husband is dear to the wife, but for the sake of the Self in the husband that the husband is dear to the wife." In other words, if a wife is attracted to her husband, she may think of him as a man but, actually speaking, it is because God Himself is there in him that she is attracted to him. Shankara, the great commentator, gave the first interpretation, and I must admit that it is closer to the language of the original Sanskrit. He says it is for her own sake that she loves the husband. That is to say, if a wife is very fond of her husband it is because of some self-interest.

It sounds hard and cynical to interpret human relationships in such terms. But if you go on analyzing your motive, you will find that even though it may not be grossly selfish, it is fundamentally selfish all the same. When a wife loves her husband fully, unselfishly, we honor such love and it is to be honored. But even then, philosophically speaking, self-interest is involved. This self gets something; some *artha*—meaning, or significance—is derived from that love. Without this significance the relationship would be untenable. A woman would not look at a man unless some value were realized by her in that person. That is true of every relationship. It is true even of the relationship between a perceiver and the material object he is perceiving. When you are looking at a mountain, or looking at the sky, or at a stone, there is some significance for you; some need of yours is being satisfied or realized in the perceiving. I would give it the simple name of self-interest.

Such self-interest may be all right in a lower state, but compared with the truth it is a deluded state. Why should you seek any significance when all significance is already within you? Somewhere a mistake has been made; otherwise all these distinctions—this is good, that is bad—would not be made. When one tries to maintain the monistic state of consciousness, spiritualizing everything, then one cannot make distinctions and differences. Therefore for a long, long time in India this practice was considered to be the religion of the *yatis*; it was called "*Yati Dharma,*" the religion of those who have formally renounced the world. Others were not taught it. But Swami Vivekananda said, "I am bringing Vedanta from the forest to the marketplace. The time has come when this truth should be spread broadcast."

Yes, though in olden days they thought it was only for the select few, now, with such widespread development of intellect, many more people can grasp this truth intellectually. However, I must admit, a peculiar situation has arisen in which our life has fallen far behind our intellectual advance, and there is therefore a kind of conflict between our intellect and our life. But this conflict will have to be eliminated; our life has to be lifted to the level of our intellectual convictions. It just won't do only to talk about these convictions while our life goes in the opposite direction. We shall somehow have to lift our life to that high level where our intellectual convictions and our living impulses become identical. This is the age in which this tremendous miracle will be accomplished. That was the faith of Swami Vivekananda. And he therefore said, "Spread all truths broadcast."

Thus many things now in our mind, in our attitudes, we shall have to gradually eliminate. For example, "This is high, this is low. Here is a saint, and here is a sinner. Here is a man, here is a woman." Do you know that when higher con sciousness grows within you it is not possible for you, or certainly it is not instinctive with you, to recognize that here is a woman and here is a man? That sense goes away. No doubt many of you are astonished to hear this. "What do you mean by that? Don't you see any more? You must admit that men look different from women. And don't you think that if you have good eyes you will recognize that difference, even if you are an illumined soul?" No. One of our great swamis, Swami Turiyananda, who lived for some years in this country, later said, "While I was in America I was not conscious of the difference between men and women." When I first heard about this, it made a very deep impression on my mind. I was then a novice in one of our monasteries, and I thought, what a wonderful thing that is: after all, there is no man, no woman in God, and if everyone is really divine you cannot say, "Here is a man, and here is a woman." To perceive the difference is a violation of the truth. You may say, "Well, it might have been a very special thing with Swami Turiyananda." Of course it is a special thing! It is not an easy thing to perceive. But I have known at least one other case in which someone realized it, or partly realized it. He himself told me, "Yes, a time comes when these distinctions, the physical appearances and all the implications of the differences between the sexes go away." As long as we have this sense of difference we must admit that we are far away from the truth. It is these errors associated with our ignorance that have to be mercilessly removed.

First of all, a strong philosophical conviction. Second, an effort to change one's outlook in practice. Every time anybody passes by remind yourself, "Here is God Himself passing in the form of this person." Afterward, you will not even say "in the form of this person," but just "God Himself passing by." Hearing a voice you will say, "God Himself is speaking." Looking at the face, looking into the eyes, you will say, "God Himself is looking through these eyes at me." " It is God who is shaking my hand." You will have to presuade yourself of these things. Next, you should destroy all the opposite tendencies, opposite convictions and instincts. They have taken the form of instincts because we have thought in the wrong way for so long.

In this connection I should tell you that most of these associated ideas arise, to begin with, from physical consciousness—physical consciousness in the sense that I think of myself as a body and other human beings as bodies. Unfortunately, most of the ideas out of which we have made so much romance and poetry are found, when traced, to have their source in body-consciousness.

A great deal of effort has to be made to rise above body-consciousness. There are demands of the body, appetites of the body. Those demands and appetites have to be denied—not fulfilled. Of course, you have paid the body its revenue for a very long time; you have fed it, clothed it, flattered it, and given it whatever it has demanded. There is a peculiar sensation in your stomach, and at once you think, "Tea time!" A few cookies and a cup of tea. What is it you have done? The body has sent you a demand and at once you have put food where the demand was. You, of course, call it four o'clock tea and say that it is but a natural thing. Actually speaking, what you have been doing is this: you have recognized yourself as the body; you have accepted the demands of the body, and you have satisfied the demands of the body. Not for nothing do all religions prescribe fasting and other kinds of abstention. The knowers of God have told us that one can meet the most rudimentary demands of the body without obstructing spiritual growth: for example, satisfy hunger enough to keep the body and soul together, enough not to get sick and so make the body an obstruction to oneself; again, supply a little protection from heat and cold. But they say no other demands of the body should be met. Now, of course, you cannot just suddenly deny all these demands at once. But by and by, by and by you will do it.

Meanwhile, you learn to look upon others not as physical but as spiritual, and you learn to look upon yourself also as Spirit. Say to yourself, "I am not the body, I am not the mind." In this way you will find you have gradually achieved victory over the body. In your country you try to accomplish such extraordinary things. I am here referring to Christian Science—a most extraordinary creed; it denies that the body has any existence. Even in India, where they have taught this monistic philosophy for ages and ages, they have not gone that far. So when I first came to know about Christian Science I could not but be impressed. You may say that many Christian Scientists do not understand the meaning of what they preach and probably do not actually practice it. But I still bow my head before the convictions of these people. Even if 99 percent fail, even if only one succeeds in a thousand, I should still honor those who hold such beliefs. It is a bold attitude to take. Of course, they make compromises. As Swami Vivekananda used to say of their teachings, "I haven't got any head, therefore let my headache go away." The Christian Scientists, of course, repudiate that kind of statement of their belief. But in practice they use their high theories for bodily ends. They say, "I am not matter, I am not body, therefore my stomachache must go. I am Spirit, therefore I should not be poor." As if money is not matter! There is a bit of self-deception there, I have to admit that. Whenever high principles are brought down to serve lower purposes, there is compromise and there is self-deception. In every religion this has taken place. A devotee says, "O Lord, You are all-powerful. I know if You wish, You can do everything for me." So he prays, sheds a few tears and at once goes out to do things for himself; he has forgotten the allpowerfulness of God. He does not say, "I said the Lord will do it for me, I shall sit quietly. Let Him do it." No, he at once goes ahead on his own. So the Lord thinks, "After all, he did not mean it, so I do not have to bother about him. Let him fend for himself." That is the way it goes. All religions when compromised become a little self-deceiving, a little contradictory. But I must say that whether Christian Scientists practice it fully or not, I have a respect for the attitude that only Spirit exists, nothing else exists.

I have sometimes thought that our whole life is governed by ideas imbibed in our childhood days. We do not accept ideas because we have tested or practiced them, but simply because they were told to us. That is to say, we are governed by opinion. Lately, I said that probably the most persuasive proof of the existence of God is the climate of opinion. The existence of God has been deeply impressed on our mind and has conditioned our thinking, conditioned our motives, our action, everything. Suppose you were to teach a child, as that great queen, Madalasa, of ancient India taught her sons, "*Tvam asi Niranjana.*" "Thou art the Pure One. Thou art Brahman, the Pure One." Taught in this way, her sons, even when they were little, became eager to find their true nature and left the world. Each told his mother, "Mother, I want to go in search of this." She replied, "Go, my son." She used to sing as she rocked the cradle, "*Tvam asi Niranjana, Tvam asi Niranjana*"; again and again she used to do that. And gradually, you see, the meaning reached them.

A child's mind is a complete mind, only it is not yet functioning completely. Just consider what tremendous learning power there is in the so-called child's mind. Within one or two years, a baby learns a whole new language. During that early period if great truths can be impressed on the child's mind, those truths will enter into its very core. I have often thought that if from their birth children did not hear such debilitating statements as, "You are a born sinner; you are a man; you are a poor man; you are a healthy man; a good man, a bad man," but were told instead, day after day, "You are eternal, you are immortal, you are ever pure, you are full of knowledge, full of strength, full of blessedness," this truth would become a power in ther lives, even when they grew up and their other instincts began to prevail.

Yes, in their lives there would be a conflict, but blessed be that conflict! A thousand blessings flow from that conflict. You people have become soft in this part of the world; you want everything just smooth and nice and pink all over. If any little conflict comes in your heart, you run to the psychiatrist. And he, poor man that he is, tries to bring you down to a lower level where you cannot think all these inconvenient, contradictory thoughts, so you become "free" from your conflict. How smooth you look now! How happy you are! But, if you are asked any serious questions, you get a headache. It is a shameful state of things. I am all for mental treatment—psychology, psychiatry, psychotherapy, everything—for actually sick men. But when I see whole men—of course, nobody is really whole, everybody has something wrong—but when I see sufficiently average men running to those people and imbibing all these stupid theories, I say, the Lord save them! Only the Lord can save them; no man can do it.

Conflict there will be. What is wrong in conflict? All growth is through conflict. You subdue your lower nature and you develop your higher nature, and eventually you eliminate the conflict—not by bringing yourself down but by raising yourself up. Suppose you say, "What happens in the meantime? In the meantine I am about to go insane." As with everything else, there is a way of doing things. If you do things rightly, you don't have to go insane. As you know, it is the parents who give the child's life an initial direction; they should teach their children how to live rightly. As it is, they teach them all the wrong things.

People have many fantastic ideas. Some parents will say, "We won't teach them any religion. We don't want to condition them." So the capacity for thinking higher thoughts disappears from their minds. They can teach them how to eat, how to sleep, how to put on clothes, but when it comes to teaching them how to be religious, teaching them about God, then they at once become ultraliberal; there they do not want to discipline their children. Yet everything thrives through discipline. In your garden you continually prune your plants, and you see how beautifully they grow, how wonderfully they bloom, what fine fruits they develop, all because you have taken care of them, disciplined them. Yet here is a life, and you do not want to do anything to it. You call it progressive education. But by the time the children grow up and conflicts come out, they are absolutely helpless, because they have never learned to control their own minds. Then the parents drag the children to the psychiatrists, if they have the money; and if they haven't they have to put them in some institution. A most shameful state of things! So I say, teach your child the noble idea that the queen taught her children. Let this sink into his life. Then, even if some conflicts come later on, you will have equipped him with the power of keeping them under control, of working against his lower instincts and eventually conquering them.

5

The spiritualizing of things has to be done by all. However, I must warn you—and when I give this warning many of you will say, "Good-bye, we don't want that!"—if you really practice seeing yourself and everyone else as divine, great detachment will come to you. If you *really* practice it. You may be married; you may have a husband, you may have children, you may have relatives, you may have friends, you may keep house, you may prepare dinner and entertain your friends, you may do all these things—but you will not be the life of the party. You see, you will find you cannot really think all these noble thoughts and get half drunk at the same time. You just cannot do it. I do not know how many friends will visit you after that. If you don't serve them cocktails and wine and all kinds of things, how many friends will you have? These are the practical difficulties. Further, you will find you cannot really engage in all the stupid talk in which most people engage; it is deadly poison, you cannot do it. Some more friends will drop out. "She has become awfully dry. She has become too religious; she is a bore." They will go away. But I say, good riddance! Probably you won't say that. I still say, good riddance! Who cares for them? Then as regards your own husband and children, your children will complain, "Mother, you are not any fun any more"; your husband will say the same thing. These are all things to take into consideration. You will have to weigh the advantages and disadvantages of this kind of philosophy and this kind of practice and take what you can.

You see, you will find you do not have the kind of attachment that you used to have. Truth is a powerful thing and the truth is: *all* are your own—not one or two select people. All are your own; everyone in the whole universe becomes your own relative. After having sung a hymn to the Divine Mother, the devotee said, "My Mother is the Goddess Pārvatī, my father is Shiva. All devotees of Shiva are my friends, and the three worlds are my own country." These are the things that will come into your mind. In the *Shrimad Bhāgavatam* it is said that when a person reaches the first stage of devotion (and don't think that is inconsiderable—that is a very high state), he doesn't care much for devotees; his mind is in God alone. When he reaches a still higher state, which has been called the middle state, he loves God but he also loves the devotees of God. And in the third stage, the highest stage, he has devotion for God, for the devotees, and for all living beings, equally.

So this detachment comes. Detachment means you are not particularly attached to someone and not attached to others. All begin to have another meaning for you. In the beginning, of course, you will not be much fun, but later you become great fun. What happens? Another quality becomes revealed through you, another quality of being; it is a strange religious phenomenon. At first all your friends and relatives oppose you and try to dissuade you; they even hate you, actually hate you with great anger in their heart. Next, they become indifferent; they have given up hope for you. Finally, they begin to be drawn towards you and to be very proud of you, talking about you, and saying, "You know, I knew him when." Very proud of you they become, with sincere pride. If you should then give up spiritual life, they would become your bitterest critics. I used to puzzle over this, until I found the answer: many things we do not possess but enjoy through others. I may not be able to sing, but if you can sing and I can hear you sing, I enjoy music thereby. So I may not have spirituality, but if you have become spiritual, I enjoy spirituality through you; and if you fail, you deprive me of something most precious, and in my disappointment I become critical of you.

A time comes, after the period of struggle is over, when a new quality reveals itself in the smile of the mother, and the children dote on her. She talks to them in a new way and there is something in it that goes deep into their hearts. The husband feels it, too, and so do the relatives and friends. True, it is not fun in the old way, but to all it is a source of attraction, and all find it good to be with her. You might say it is too good to be true. Well, I don't think it is too good to be true, I think it is good and equally true. You just have to practice this, and you will find that people who have a little worth in them will come like bees to a full-blown flower to sip the honey. Afterwards, in fact, this attraction becomes an obstruction for the spiritual man. A wonderful beauty of appearance and of character comes, and it is a source of such tremendous attraction that all kinds of people are drawn to him. Of course, those who are attracted are benefited; but the spiritual person himself cannot find the peace and quiet and solitude necessary for spiritual practice. So for a period he has to run away and live by himself.

For a wife or mother who has reached this stage, nothing is secular any more , and this gives rise to certain difficulties. Very soon she will find sexual life ends for her. It cannot last because it would be contrary to the Spirit. The husband may not like it; a special attachment, naturally expected between husband and wife, goes out of their life. It is replaced by something very deep; it is like a blessing. But I must admit that to the ordinary man it will not seem right; the old attachment is gone, and habits are changed. But to the person who is practicing this spiritualizing of everything, it is a most wonderful life. Every moment is a moment of worship. If you have prepared your husband's dinner, that is worship. To whom are you going to offer it? You do not even say "to God in man." Rather, you would then say "to God Himself." Is it for your children you are preparing dinner? Again, it is an offering to God Himself. If you are washing their clothes, mending their clothes, you are serving the Lord. You will be conscious of it; and therefore every moment becomes instinct with the consciousness of God.

You see what has happened here: your whole waking life has become one continual spiritual practice. I sometimes speak of it as continuous meditation, for you could not maintain this spirit and this attitude and this intense sense of worshipfulness unless your mind were in a deep state, which is the state of meditation. No one superficial can ever practice this. Everything that you do is a form of worship. Everyone that you see is God

Himself; you are having a continuous vision of God.

Sometimes people ask, "When shall I see God? Where is God? Where is the proof that God exists?" All these questions arise from utter foolishness, because whatever you are seeing at this moment is God Himself. This whole universe and everything in it is God Himself. Are you really seeing anything else? If you think so, in your evaluation you are making a mistake. You have come to a field where all kinds of pebbles are scattered about. You are in search of diamonds. You pick one up—throw it away; pick another up—throw it away. Every pebble you picked up was a diamond. You did not recognize it as such, so you just dropped it. Then you said, "I could not find any diamonds."

You are seeking God. God is present before you in this form, in that form; everyone is God. That is why Swami Vivekananda said, "Do not seek Him, just see Him." Rub your eyes, clear your vision; you are not seeing clearly. You do not have to seek Him, because He is here; nothing else but God is present here. Whether living or nonliving, human or subhuman—it is God Himself. What is wanted is that we see Him clearly. Then we find our satisfaction.

So this is what the life of a spiritual aspirant is. I should end by saying this: It is not that a person is always active, you know. The mother we are thinking of is not all the time cooking and cleaning and washing and so on. Then what does she do? Maybe she sits down; maybe she reads the scriptures. Maybe she just *is*, and that is the state of meditation. The mind of such a person, man or woman, cannot dwell on anything except on God. So when there is no outward activity, the mind will plunge into the meditative consciousness of God.

Yes, that is it. When you close your eyes you see God. When you open your eyes you see God. That is the ideal. If you don't like the usual ritualistic worship, then practice this that I have described today, worship God in man. Or, if you like, practice both. Be holy, be pure. Don't be gross. God is the finest of the fine and to gross-minded people He never comes, rest assured of that. If you say, "Well, then there is no hope for us." Why not? You are also fine. But you want to indulge in all kinds of grossness. You want to have the pleasure and the fun of becoming gross: eating this, eating that; going here, going there; dressing this way, dressing that way; pandering to the appetites of the body all the time. You want to have that fun and yet want to be spiritual. You cannot do it. You cannot worship God and mammon. But if you want, you can become free of this desire for the gross. That is why I don't hesitate to say all these discouraging things; I know that in you there is the power of rising above all grossness. And when you do, your finer nature will manifest itself.

Let me tell you, these are very propitious times. When the summer comes, or when the spring season is in full swing, you can sow any seed anywhere and it will sprout and grow; in the same way, this is the time in which any spiritual effort will become immensely blessed, immensely fruitful. A little effort and you will get results. Yes, there are also winter seasons in the history of man, and then whatever you do is of no avail. But this, it so happens, is the spring, spring in full swing, and so why should you not try?

1. See *Complete Works of Swami Vivekananda,* 8:433 (9th ed.)
2. *Bṛhadāraṇyka Upaniṣad,* 4.5.6

WORSHIP OF THE SPIRIT
BY THE SPIRIT

WORSHIP OF THE SPIRIT BY THE SPIRIT

1

These words "Worship of the Spirit by the Spirit" I have taken from a lecture given by Swami Vivekananda in San Francisco entitled "Is Vedanta the Future Religion?" In that lecture the Swami spoke from a rather extreme point of view and deliberately disparaged the ritualistic worship undertaken in temples and churches. He pointed out that man is Spirit, God is Spirit, both are formless and perfect, and the true worship is worship of the Spirit by the Spirit.

In the Swami's mind was the idea, I think—and most of us will accept it on self-examination—that dualistic worship is usually undertaken for some gain on earth or in heaven, not for God's own sake. One can easily understand why it is so: As a devotee you usually think of yourself as an average human being, having human qualities, both positive and negative, and human aspirations. And because you feel you cannot get what you are seeking by ordinary means, or because you are afflicted by great crises from time to time for which you can see no human remedy, you approach God. You think He is all-powerful and compassionate, all-merciful and all love; therefore He will grant you what you want. Yes, it is a sad commentary on human nature that, whatever may be the form of our religion, most of us worship God for selfish reasons.

Even that kind of worship, however, is not altogether wrong. As Sri Krishna points out in the *Bhagavad-Gita,* there are four kinds of devotees of God: the first class, *ārta,* includes those who are in distress and approach God for help; the second, *jijñāsu,* those who are inquiring after spiritual truths or after the nature of God, as, for example, students of philosophy; the third, *arthārthī,* those who seek things of God, such as prosperity in this life, cure of diseases, or heavenly life after death; and the fourth class, *jñānī,* those who have knowledge of God, who know Him as He really is. Since they all have been considered devotees, those who seek worldly things from God are not to be condemned; we must know, however, that such seeking is only a beginning. If religion is understood as something by professing which and practicing which we are able to realize eternal truths, then seeking worldly things from God is not much of a religion.

Now, the reason we undertake such dualistic worship is that we think of ourselves in our own naive terms as physical and mental beings possessing an immortal soul. We express this attitude by saying "my soul," and "his soul"; whereas the truth is we *are* the soul. Actually, our expressions "my body" or "my mind" are more true to fact. If you say "my body" or "my mind," what is this 'I'? It could not possess a body and mind and also *be* the body and mind. So there you are right, for you are assuming you are the soul, the Spirit, which is different from the body and the mind. Why, then, do you say at the same time "my soul," "his soul," "their souls," and so on? Our mode of speaking shows that we are in a peculiar state of confusion. We contradict ourselves. As long as we think of ourselves as being physical and mental, possessing a soul, we shall have dualistic forms of worship, and we shall ask of God things conducive to the well-being and comfort of body and mind. Most religions, we must admit, are busy with these things.

What is the wonder, then, that Swami Vivekananda, while speaking about Vedanta and thinking and feeling in the strain in which he most often taught, should speak critically of some of these dualistic forms of religion? Yet he also wrote books and gave lectures on dualistc religion; further, he taught that one should not condemn any form of religion. Sri Ramakrishna, the Master of Swami Vivekananda, had believed in all the different paths by which the soul progresses towards God—dualism, qualified monism, and monism or nondualism; he had practiced all kinds of religions and from his personal experience had found them all to be true. But both Sri Ramakrishna and Swami Vivekananda recognized that although one starts with dualism one does not end with it, for it blends into qualified monism, which, in turn, gradually leads to and ends in monism. To stop with dualism, that is the mistake. Moreover, while neither Swami Vivekananda nor his Master condemned dualism, they did condemn the seeking of worldly things from God. Neither of them could tolerate that.

The Swami would sometimes illustrate the point with Sri Ramakrishna's example of the rich man. When you visit a rich man he is flattered but knows that you really don't care for him, you are only trying to get something out of him; as soon as you get it you will leave him, or even if you don't get it you will leave him. But once a certain rich man asked a person who frequented his house, "Now, what do you want?" The visitor replied, "Sir, I don't want anything. I like you; therefore I come to see you." And the rich man was highly pleased. When we approach God most of us ask things of Him. Of course, even then, God is pleased a little—at least you have remembered Him. Although you came to Him for the sake of getting something out of Him, at least you looked at His face. In a sense God's position is not enviable, is it? People come to see Him not for His own sake but for what they can get out of Him. Nobody likes to be placed in that position. Nevertheless, those who have known God say that even if a person thinks of Him momentarily and approaches Him, no matter what his purpose, God is thereby pleased. But He is not *highly* pleased; there is regret that the devotee did not ask anything better of Him.

Well, most people ask for material things, but there are some who do not. If you study those who don't, you will find that although their language and their initial approach may be dualistic, they are truly monistic. They say, "I do not see any difference between me and my Lord," or, "I cannot bear any separation between my Lord and me," Don't you see? The very nature of devotion is to gravitate towards the object of devotion. Wherever there is true love, there comes at-onement. If somebody says to a true devotee, "O devotee, you will always remain separate from God," it will break his heart. He will reply, "Please don't tell me such a thing; I cannot bear it! I want to embrace my Lord, to blend into Him. I want to surrender myself completely to Him!" A monist will reply to such an outburst, "Well, what is the sense, then, in your believing in dualism? After all, dualism is the very thing you are objecting to!" Yes, at-onement with God is the true ideal of a dualist, and since that is so, he might as well use a little more logical language and call himself a monist.

The trouble is that people don't like to be called monists. The general criticism of monism by devotees is, "Oh, that is so dry!" Why should it be dry? After all, the monists say that Brahman is *Sat-cit-ānanda,* Infinite Being, Infinite Truth, Infinite Joy. The fact is that monism, in order to explain itself, to establish its truth, has had to take recourse to logical language. If you declare that this world does not exist, this world is false, and the individual is the Infinite God, you have to give arguments to bolster such terrible and preposterous statements. The language of the arguments is very logical, and logical language naturally has to be rather dry. You cannot make it juicy, because then it is bound to become illogical. Your opponents will pounce upon everything you say: "What did you mean by this word? Verify that statement! You contradict yourself!"

I would not say that dualists have not also used logical language, but they eat their cake and have it too. You will find, if you study dualistic religions, that they have a beautiful facade of emotional language, which their adherents say is their religion; then, in order to support and defend it, they have a thesis which is called a theology, because it is not much of a philosophy. And theologies are full of complex logic. If you have to explain something that is not altogether true, you have to spin out awfully subtle and complicated things to justify it. So I do not see the difficulty about dryness in monism; both paths, you see, can be dry, and both can also be full of emotion and feeling. There is a monism, for example, which is the very essence of love. If love means at-onement, then that identity which is the goal and the truth of monism will be the highest love. Why should it not be? Why should we always think that monism is just logic, something dry? It also can be approached from the standpoint of emotion. The only difference is that the goal of monism will never be less than complete at-onement of the soul and Brahman.

2

All these things were back of the thought of Swami Vivekananda when, in course of the lecture to which I referred, he spoke of monism as the future religion and asked us to worship the Spirit by the Spirit. I would like to examine some phases of that kind of worship and the truths that are implied by "worship of the Spirit by the Spirit."

I think these words will remind you of some words in the Gospel of John. There it is said, "God is a Spirit: and they that worship him must worship him in spirit and in truth."[2] Whenever I remember that passage I also remember the story in which this saying of Jesus occurs. Jesus told the most profound things to—of all people—a Samaritan woman who was inferior in both education and moral character, at least from a worldly point of view. Christ had come to the well from which the Samaritan woman was drawing water and asked her to give him a drink. And he said that if she knew who was asking for water, she would have asked him for the water of life. Then the whole thing opened up. He knew somehow that this woman was living an immoral life, and when he mentioned it she openly admitted it. And he started telling her about this idea of worship. He told her that the time was coming when God would be worshiped neither in the mountain of Samaria, where the Samaritans worshiped, nor in the temple of Jerusalem, where the Jews worshiped, and he said, "The hour cometh and now is, when the true worshipers shall worship the Father in spirit and in truth: for the Father seeketh such to worship him. God is a Spirit: and they that worship him must worship him in spirit and in truth."[3]

You might ask here: In what sense did Christ, as he is presented in the Gospel of John, use this word *spirit*? Did he use it to denote a thing that is immaterial but may have some form, as we use the word even today for the ghost of a departed person? In those days, also, this was one of the senses in which they used the word. But Christ said that the spirit is like the wind. His meaning was that spirit had no form and, further, that it was spontaneous—"it bloweth where it listeth, . . . whence it cometh and whither it goeth"[4] nobody knows—there was no method about it. It is also to be noted in this comparison that spirit is known by its function, its action, just as we know the wind by its function. The wind makes the trees and other things move, and thereby we know of its presence. But we do not see it nor can we say how it is going to behave.

So here was the picture of spirit—of God as spirit: He was formless, but He functioned; He was unpredictable—He could not be governed by ordinary laws; He had a free will, and nobody could say how He would work. Actually, by using the illustration of the wind Christ does not give any very extraordinary idea of God as spirit. But that was not the purpose of the Christ; his purpose was to give the idea of the spirit as a dynamic entity—as formless and yet with power.

Now, what did Christ mean by worshiping God in spirit and in truth? Probably most Christians find it easier to understand what is meant by *truth* than by *spirit*. For instance, in another quotation from John, "Ye shall know the truth and the truth shall make you free,"[5] the word *spirit* does not occur, and many commentators have said that the truth is this: Christ is the Savior, God is merciful, and if you believe in Christ, you will enter into the kingdom of heaven. But in the quotation in which we are told to worship God in spirit and in truth, these two ideas, spirit and truth, have been brought together. What does Christ mean by this? What does he mean by worshiping God in spirit?

Well, Swami Vivekananda would say this means recognizing *yourself* as Spirit. Some of you may say, "No, we are to worship God by knowing *Him* to be Spirit." But since Christ first said that God is a Spirit and then said that He should be worshiped in spirit and in truth, he certainly meant to give another idea by the second use of the word *spirit*. So it must be as Swami Vivekananda would interpret it: worship God, feeling that He is Spirit and you are Spirit. That would be the truth— the truth about yourself and the truth about God. Thus, if you worship Him in this way you will be worshiping Him in Spirit and in Truth; in your worship there will be no element of falsehood or unreality. If, on the other hand, you do not recognize Him as Spirit and if you do not recognize yourself as Spirit, your worship of Him is not the truest worship. Just as worshiping God in an idol or thinking of Him only as an object of formal worship would not be to worship Him in truth, in the same way, to worship Him without thinking of *yourself* as Spirit would not be to worship Him "in spirit and in truth."

When you study Vedanta philosophy and are convinced of the truth of its teachings, the whole thing becomes clear. Of course God is Spirit. As I have already told you, Vedantists call Him *Sat-cit-ānanda,* and part of His name, *Cit,* means Spirit. He is beyond all forms, physical or mental, and beyond all dualities and multiplicities—the pure Spirit. Now, when we speak of ourselves as Spirit, the word is generally used in a negative way: we have to grasp the meaning of Spirit by contrasting it with body and mind, by saying it is not the body, it is not the mind, but something different from and much finer than the body and the mind.

You know the doctrine of the five sheaths that

Vedantists speak of. In regard to the individual there is first, starting from the most external aspect, this physical sheath, Then there is the vital sheath, the sheath of life. Life is a peculiar thing, belonging to both mind and body. I am using this word *life* not so much in the scientific sense as in a more general and philosophical sense. The word in our philosophical texts is *prāna,* which is ordinarily translated as "life force." (Philosophically, it would be better to translate it as "energy," living or nonliving; it may even indicate mechanical energy, but we won't go into that now.) Life pervades this body, we know that. But life also pervades the mind, every aspect of the mind. Thus, our philosophers speak of this life force as the vital sheath. Then comes the mental sheath; next the sheath which is spoken of as the knowledge or intelligence sheath; and last the blissful sheath.

Now, these last three sheaths are all phases of the mind—fine, finer, and yet finer phases. Even in our present experience we have an idea of these phases in a crude sort of way. When various thoughts arise in the mind, we have an idea of the mental sheath, that part of our being in which this movement of thought takes place. The knowledge or intelligence sheath is that in which judgments and conclusions are arrived at, where reason functions and intelligent propositions flash. And when we have joy, happiness, pleasure, for whatever reason, it rises in another part of the mind, and that is called the blissful sheath.

But when I say we have an idea of these phases, you must understand that when you are tied up with the mental sheath, vital sheath, and physical sheath—when you dwell essentially in these sheaths—then you know the intelligence sheath and the blissful sheath as through a mist or fog; you do not know them clearly. Yes, we know that intelligence functions within us, but in our present state we cannot know pure intelligence, intelligence as it is in itself. Take a tyrant, a dictator drunk with power. He will order around a great man—for instance, a great scholar—and treat him like a nobody. Would you say that he has a true understanding of the scholar or scientist? No. He will say, "Why, I have many scientists as my servants; they obey my orders." But how could he understand what a scientist is? He is after all just an ignorant tyrant. We are treating the better part of our mind in the same way. We treat our intelligence and bliss from our low point of view. That is why our intelligence is at the mercy of our senses and of our imperfect knowledge; and that is why the fruit of our thinking is not always worthwhile but often shot through and through with error. If, however, we let the intelligence and bliss that we have within us function in their own way, we will be surprised at their luminous character. When intelligence regains its freedom, it will take us immediately to the highest truth. Only by renunciation and meditation can we grant this liberation to intelligence and to joy. Otherwise, they are the servants of our senses and even of our thoughts; they are not functioning as they are in themselves.

Intelligence is so fine a part of the mind, so free, that a person who lives in the liberated intelligence feels himself incorporeal, limitless. He does not feel tied down by this small body. There is almost a sense of omniscience and a sense of eternity about him. And notice, all this is in the mind. If you want to say that you are beyond the body and mind, just imagine how much you have to realize and how much you have to set aside! If you have to set aside even liberated intelligence and liberated joy, just imagine what the Spirit must be! It is through such comparisons that you can understand what the Spirit is. The *Taittirīya Upaniṣad* gives this kind of comparative understanding of the nature of the soul in the last two of its three chapters. These are called "Brahmananda Valli" and "Ananda Valli"—the "Book of the Joy of Brahman" and the "Book of Joy."

And you *are* the Spirit. You are neither this body nor this mind. Why should this be called the truth? Because it is invariable. Truth is that which does not change; truth is that which is not dependent. If it were dependent, it would change when that upon which it depends changes. Look at a rainbow on a waterfall; if the sun changes or the position of the water changes, your rainbow disappears. The rainbow changes because it is dependent. Everything is as dependent as the rainbow as long as we live the way we are living. Therefore, the facts of our present existence cannot be called true. Oh, I know some of you will say, "But they are relatively true, aren't they? Wouldn't you say they are true under certain conditions?" But why should I use the word *true* to indicate something that is not true? Well, of course, if you cannot find any other convenient word and want to use the word *true*, I have no objection to it, but let us understand that we are using the same word to indicate completely different things. Truth, correctly speaking, has to have eternity about it, everlastingness. And the moment you realize this, you have to think that it is unconditioned, independent, limitless. Therefore, the two phrases "in spirit" and "in truth" really mean the same thing, only they draw our attention to it from two different points of view.

You might ask, "Did Christ really use the word *spirit* in that sense? Well, who knows in what sense he used it, and how can anyone know? Even about the authorship of the Gospel of John there are all kinds of doubts. But one of the characteristics of the words of illumined persons, particularly of prophets and saints, is that they have to be interpreted differently under different conditions. Their words have a tendency of revealing greater and greater depths of significance, and it is desirable, nay, it is necessary, that we reinterpret their great messages as time passes and conditions change. If we do not do this, we do not do them proper justice.

The great truths that come down to us serve two purposes: they are revelations of eternal verities, and they fill the needs of the particular age in which they are first uttered. When the next age comes, you will probably find that their temporal meaning is no longer applicable. But if you then reject them, you will do injustice to them as revelations of eternal truths. So the necessity of reinterpretation is great. However, I myself do not believe I am reinterpreting Christ's words; I believe I am giving you the correct interpretation when I say that by "in truth" he was really referring to the same thing as "in spirit." Take the saying, "Ye shall know the truth, and the truth shall make you free." That is purely Vedantic. Actually, there is nowhere in this statement any idea that you will be free only when you take recourse to Christ. Christ also said, "Blessed are the pure in heart, for they shall see God."[6] It is just like that.

Once a Christian missionary in India met one of our monks and of course beat the same old missionary drum: "Oh, you cannot have salvation unless you become a Christian." "Why?" asked the monk and quoted the Bible: "In the Gospel it is said, 'Blessed are the pure in heart, for they shall see God.' There is no other condition laid down there."

Of course the missionary could not say anything. No doubt the theologians would have some explanation: "First of all you become pure in heart, and as a result you learn about the Savior; then you take refuge in the Savior and you will see God—not in this life, though—after you die." But that is the role of theologians and commentators. They are always wiser than the prophets and even than God Himself.

The same kind of interpretation of the scriptures goes on in India. Sri Krishna says in the *Bhagavad-Gita,* a compendium of his teachings, that there are two approaches to truth; one is through *jñāna,* (knowledge) and the other through karma (action). He tells how men have found truth by following the path of *sānkhya,* that is, *jñāna,* and also by following the path of karma. He gives the illustration of King Janaka and others who attained God by practicing *karma yoga.* But when these words of the Lord fell into the hands of the commentator Shankara, who always fought the idea that work will take one to the truth, he said, "Oh, no! What is meant here is that those who follow the path of action in the right spirit become purified; then they take to the path of contemplation or *jñāna* and realize God." That is the commentator for you. Well, however that may be, I think there is always a necessity of going back to the original text. Temporal needs change, and through such change of needs we sometimes submerge valuable meanings. Then, turning to the original, we again become aware of the basic truths; we rediscover them.

3

A great change has to be brought about within oneself in order to worship God "in spirit and in truth." I have often given you a sort of formula in regard to this change. You see, there are three things correlated: the knower, the subject; the state of mind, which is the instrument of perception; and the object of knowledge—the world and God. These three are all tied together; they are parts or aspects of one entity. So if changes occur in one of them, there is simultaneous change in the other two. Now, ordinarily, the mind is so engrossed in concrete objects like the body and things of the physical world that its own correlated condition may be called a condition of scatteredness: there is continual movement and restlessness. Conversely, if this mind is restless, then as a result, you perceive yourself as a psychophysical being, with emphasis on the physical; outside reality appears as physical reality, and as regards God, you would not even dream of thinking about Him. It is no wonder, therefore, that those who have convinced themselves that their present state of mind and mode of knowledge are ultimate do not want to think of God. And it is no wonder that you are becoming godless people. You could not be otherwise: if the mind is scattered, then you will think yourselves to be psychophysical beings and the world a material world. No God, no spirit; God and spirit are all just meaningless talk. In fact, nowadays you are taught to forget all these things; they are said to unnecessarily clutter and confuse your mind.

But let this mind be a little more quiet. What would you feel then? When a little quietness comes into the mind, you feel you are a soul—not Spirit yet, but something a little different from the mind and the body. You will actually have that feeling. If you say, "Well, *some* people may have such a feeling, but not I," I tell you, everybody will have it; if there has been a little change in the condition of the mind, this consciousness will come. And when you look at others, you will begin to feel that they, too, are a little more than mere body and mind. You will see something else there. You do not have to infer it; you actually feel it. When you look at the world, you will feel that behind this material world is a finer entity, and God will not seem so unreal or impossible as He seemed before.

Let the mind become still finer; say it becomes really quiet. Then, although you will not yet feel yourself as altogether separate from the body and the mind, you will be convinced that you are a separate entity. When you look at other people, you will not think, "Here is a man, here is a woman." The body might be female or male, but back of it is a being which is neither. You will not merely feel, you will begin to perceive that this universe is not a material universe at all but is pervaded by something else, something much more wonderful than the mind or body or anything of the mind or body. And God will seem very close to you—real, interpenetrating everything. You will feel like sitting quiet and perceiving Him here, in the heart. This is where the perception comes, in the heart; the brain is just a receiving station. Haven't you noticed that when you see even the most beautiful scenery outside, enjoyment of it is here in the heart? This is where everything is gathered. It is in the heart you feel the presence of God, and feeling it, you just close your eyes. You want to feel Him deeper; you want to feel Him more and more. All these things come to you.

Eventually, when the mind has become completely calm and you become completely separated from body and mind, you will even forget their existence. You will forget the existence of this world. All that you will perceive will be one undivided Spirit, having neither interior nor exterior. What interior or exterior can there be if you have forgotten your own body? What you perceive then cannot be spoken about or even conceived in terms of our present experience.

Now, I have described the changes that take

place when the condition of your mind changes, but there are other ways of speaking of it. Suppose your heart has gone to God and you perceive only Him. Then your mind will become quiet; and all the rest will follow just as I have told you. Or suppose you reason, "I am not the body, I am not the mind," and you perceive youself to be Spirit. Then, too, the mind will become quiet and the world will appear as spiritual. That is to say, if a change takes place in any one of these three aspects of existence—the knower, the instrument of knowledge, and the object of knowledge— the other two aspects will simultaneously change, since they are all tied up together.

So, whatever my path may be, I try to realize the truth, that eternal Reality which never changes. I transcend the idea that I am the body and the mind and try to establish myself in the Spirit. Therefore, when I worship God, what shall I seek of Him? If I am inclined towards the path of reason, I shall try to lose myself in this inscrutable Being; I won't talk about love or any such thing. But if I approach Him from the standpoint of love or devotion, I shall feel myself also to be infinite love, infinite joy, and I shall lose myself in this infinite love and infinite joy. And that is worship of the Spirit by the Spirit.

4

You can see from what I have said that an essential part of this worship is continual self-transcendence. We have an instinctive sense of self which we have to analyze carefully to see if in this self are mixed up the ingredients of matter and mind. Continually, you have to watch it. And how do you watch it? First of all, watch your own feelings. You feel you are tired? Then say, "No, I am not tired. Body may be tired; I am not tired." You do not allow that sense of tiredness to be reflected in your consciousness. Mind might be feeling this, that, or the other thing, but you say, "I am not any of those things." Deny to these conditions of the mind the right to become a part of yourself. Affirm continually the free nature of your own true being and remain in that consciousness. You have to be very watchful, very watchful! For a long time, in spite of your watchfulness, all these foreign elements will creep into your consciousness. But what of it? Don't you know that once you have taken a stand, it is just a question of time before your resolution asserts itself fully over everything? But you must stand your ground; you must not yield. You must not say, "This philosophy doesn't work. Being tired may be only a condition of the body, but just the same I feel *I* am tired, too." Don't be so cowardly! Strong people will fight many battles before they win a victory.

When the powerful Emperor Akbar, the greatest of the Moguls, was reigning in Delhi, he was resisted by many kings of small Rajput kingdoms. These Rajputs were great fighters, with a high code of honor. Akbar, who was a very extraordinary man, found that the only way of settling the hostility between the Rajput kings and the Mogul empire was to enter into matrimonial alliances with them; so he began to marry the daughter of one, the sister of another, and so on. He also gave Rajputs very high positions in his court; some of them he made generals, others, finance ministers. Not all of the kings, however, yielded to Akbar. Rana Pratap Singh, the ruler of the Rajputana kingdom of Udaipur, said, "No! I shall never submit to the Mohammedan emperor." And he would have nothing to do with those who did submit. Of course Akbar's armies attacked his capital city, Chitor, and captured it.

There is a beautiful story about this event. Some blacksmiths lived in Chitor, and their function was to make weapons for Rana Pratap. When the city was taken by the Mohammedans and the king had to flee, this whole community of blacksmiths also left the city, and they vowed, "We shall never reenter this city until it again comes into our possession." The Moguls kept Chitor until they were defeated by the British, who then became its rulers. The blacksmiths became a migratory community. They would move from place to place, taking their tools in their carts and making little things for the villagers. Do you know when they reentered Chitor? Almost four hundred years later; for not until Indian independence did it come back to the hands of the Rajputs. There was a great reception for them in the city, and now they are settling down there. Such was the spirit of the Rajputs.

When Rana Pratap left Chitor, he was driven with his queen and their little son from place to place, place to place. He had nothing; they were harassed and impoverished. One day when they didn't have anything to eat Rana Pratap gathered some grass seeds, and his queen baked some bread out of them; but an animal came and ate up the bread. And the child, hungry, began to cry. That broke the heart of the great king. So he wrote a letter to Akbar and said, "I shall accept your terms. I shall pay homage to you. I shall accept your sovereignty." There was a Rajput prince and poet living in the court. He saw the letter; and at once he said, "Ah! All this time, although we ourselves proved cowards, we were still proud of our race because of Rana Pratap. Now that he is submitting, we have lost everything." He wrote a beautiful letter in verse to Rana Pratap in which he expressed the agony of his heart. It has become very famous, that letter. But even before Rana Pratap received it, he had written again to Akbar, withdrawing his submission. And then he fought and fought and fought until he had won back part of his kingdom, and Akbar recognized that he would never be able to defeat him.

Yes, my friends, we have to be greater even than Rana Pratap if we want to win this inner victory. If you want to find yourself, to realize yourself as the Spirit, you will have to fight thousands of battles. Religion is for the strong always, not for the weak. Whether strength comes to you in the name of your own inner nature or in the name of God, strength there has to be. And it is much better if we start with the idea that we are strong. There need not be any pride or egotism about it; a strong man is not necessarily an egotist. A cowardly man is more egotistical than a strong man. The strong are gentle by nature and unselfconscious; it is the small man whose ego is easily hurt. We have to win many victories. Don't admit defeat. Even if you find that nothing is left for you, even then stand your ground, bide your time, and at the first opportunity raise your head. That is the thing you have to do.

Yes, slowly and slowly those changes I have described will come. Only a calm, serene mind can watch the processes of the mind. Remember that the mind is not yourself. It is very devious, and although it has many wonderful qualities, for a long time it will be your enemy. So watch it! Watch and see that the things you are rejecting are not coming in another form into your mind and being accepted by you. Afterwards you will find that you have become free of the mind, you have become its master.

That time will come. You will really feel when you are eating, you are not eating; it has nothing to do with you. Everything that you do, it has nothing to do with you. Food, drink, sleep, fatigue—all sorts of actions and states come, but these are nothing to you; everything leaves you untouched, because Spirit is your true nature. Why should you dance to every tune—you, the sovereign Spirit? Gradually you begin to feel the presence of that sovereign Spirit everywhere, and then, if by temperament you are devotionally inclined, you find that this perception is true devotion. You don't ask anything else of God—comfort for the body, a cure for this, that, or the other thing. Only one thing wells out of your heart—a great attraction to God—and you find you are drawn towards Him. Only love comes out of your heart, and that love is true love. I myself am conviced that as long as a man thinks that he is even the mind, his love will not be pure but will be mixed up with other considerations. Rightly speaking, as Sri Krishna said, the greatest of all the Lord's devotees is the *jñāni*. He who has found the truth is the true devotee.

5

You may wonder whether, in addition to the

practice I have described, there is any ritualism or other kind of practice to be undertaken in worshiping the Spirit by the Spirit. Yes, there is an outer as well as an inner practice.

But before speaking of the outer practice, I should point out that the inner practice has two forms: negating that which is unspiritual, and affirming the Spirit. In affirming the Spirit, remember that you are not the only Spirit; everyone is Spirit. Affirm this truth always, wheresoever you look. As long as you recognize body and mind and give value to them, you will be in the fog of ignorance. You must say that behind body and mind is Spirit. The true man is not the speaking man nor the eating, sleeping, dancing man. All these things are being done by the not-Self.

You see, we have an idea that we are doing things or that the soul is doing them. No, the soul or Spirit has nothing to do with it. In the *Gita,* the Lord himself said, "All work is performed by the *guṇas* of *prakṛti* (nature or matter). But he whose mind is deluded by egotism thinks, 'I am the doer.' "[7] But while the soul or Spirit has nothing to do with action, it has somehow drunk deep of the wine of egotism and has become so confused that it thinks it is doing everything. You generally find that when you have become a little separated from the body, when the mind has become a little calm, then you realize that the true state is actionlessness. All of us think we have to do things, do things, do things! The world will go to pieces unless we do things! The truth is that the world is going to pieces *because* we do things. Let us stop doing things—in the right way of course—and we shall see whether the world goes to pieces or becomes unified. We have all kinds of stupid ideas which we never examine, and we shout and howl and run like a pack of wolves, without rhyme or reason. But learn to be a little quiet, and you will understand. When you begin to catch a glimpse of yourself as separate from the body and the mind—just a glimpse—you will understand the truth of action and inaction. You will feel, regarding yourself, that you are the Spirit, and regarding others, that they also are the Spirit. That is part of the worship.

You must look upon others as Spirit just as you look upon yourself; otherwise there is great danger that egotism will come back to you in a subtle form. You should avoid making your spiritual practice self-bound, concerned with yourself alone. That is why you find almost all dualistic religions advise their followers to practice charity and be kind to others. Chaitanya said to the worshipers of the Lord, "Be kind to all living beings and serve the devotees." Why? Because, you see, devotional practices are bound to be self-centered. You love God and want to forget everything else. You say, "Oh, don't disturb me." Just like any lover who wants to be by himself and think of the beloved, you don't want any interference. If someone comes and asks a lover what is the matter, he says, "Don't talk to me now, don't talk to me now!" A devotee is just like that. So in Christianity, for example, you are expected to serve others because all Christians are integral parts of the Church of Christ; if you just stand alone and pay no heed to the other members of the Church, you are wrong. We can see psychologically why it has to be so.

In the path of *jñāna* there is the same danger. A time comes when the world disappears—the world *is* unreal and the Self is Brahman; that is the truth. But when you are still seeing the world, it will not do to say that the world is unreal. There is always a danger that you will dry up within and become egotistical: So what is the answer? Teachers of this path will tell you to say, "If I am the Spirit, you also, my friends, are this infinite Spirit." From that understanding, service will follow when service is called for. This looking upon both yourself and others as Spirit is the inner practice of *jñāna.*

The external practice—external worship of the Spirit by the Spirit—consists of serving God in man. Yes, that is what Swami Vivekananda recommended—actual service. Now, this kind of worship does not preclude worshiping God in a shrine or chapel; there is no harm in that , because God exists there, too, and you can worship Him in any way you like. But in addition to formal worship there must be this other kind of which I am speaking: wherever you see the Spirit, render your service and worship there.

How do you worship God in man? In whichever form God appears, respond to Him accordingly. We have a saying in India that if He apppears as a horse, give Him oats. If he appears in the guise of a sick man, bring medicine and proper diet and nurse Him. If he comes as a hungry man, give Him food. If He comes as an ignorant man, give Him intellectual knowledge. That is worship. You are not doing these things for others out of pity. I admit that pitying a person is better than being hardhearted towards him, but if you have developed beyond that hardhearted stage, you have to know a truer way than pity of responding to the Spirit. If you don't know how to respond, you should learn. You see, those who know God learn through their intimate acquaintance with Him how to respond to His infinite moods. If you study the lives of those who live in great intimacy with God, you will see how He manifests Himself in the hearts of His devotees in infinitely different ways, inconceivable to us in our present state. And you also see how the devotees respond to those moods of God.

Some people have asked me—"Well, after you have achieved *samādhi* and God-vision, then what? Is there nothing left to do?" This is what you do: you know God in His infinite ways. There is no end, no end, no end as long as you live in time—no end to His manifestations. Intimate manifestations. There is a sport. It is called the sport of the soul with God. We get some idea of it by studying the lives of great knowers of God, great lovers of God, who are intimate with Him. And, as I said, we who are in the lower stages can also learn from them how to respond to His moods.

If it pleases him to appear before me as an angry man, I learn to soothe Him, to be gentle and respond to Him in a kindly way. Not because of fear or any such thing, but because if the Lord chooses to show His angry face to me, this is the way I should respond. If He comes in the form of a thief, I shall call the police—very kindly, of course. Yes, such things have happened too, though generally the knowers of God avoid this sort of situation. But you know there are better situations. You meet all kinds of people, and if you want to have an external practice in the worship of the Spirit by the Spirit, such service is that practice.

Well, of course this worship is great fun. As I have already mentioned, it does not exclude the recognized form of worship in chapels and shrines and so on. There is no contradiction, because God is not merely manifested in human beings but can also manifest Himself on an altar. He can manifest Himself formlessly or with form, in an idol or an image, in a symbol, or in empty space. There is a shrine in one of the very well-known temples of shrine in one of the very well-known temples of South India where the Lord has manifested Himself in formless space, *ākāsa.* There is a screen in front of the shrine room, and when devotees congregate to have a vision of this holy of holies, the temple priests remove the screen and reveal empty space. That is His shrine; that is His image or symbol. In other places He has manifested Himself as water; in a spring, for example, there is the presence of God. Everywhere there are manifestations. You are not bound by the doctrines of this philosophy to recognize God only in human form. It doesn't have to be. But I must admit that this is where the emphasis is.

So, then, as time goes on, you recognize the presence of the Spirit in every being, including yourself. Your mind has quieted down. You have become free of the bondages of the body and the mind, and therefore you have become aware of the presence of this undivided, infinite Spirit everywhere, within and without. And out of you arises a strong desire to become unified with It. You know that you have left behind those things which are unstable, temporal; you are getting more and more established in truth. You feel that you are becoming Spirit, eternal Spirit. There is still a distinction between Spirit outside yourself and within yourself, and there is a tremendous mutual attraction. And then the two become one, and the worship has come to an end.

That is the worship of the Spirit by the Spirit. It is the only religion worthy of the dignity of a human being. If a person feels that he is a strong being, a pure being, that is the one worthy religion. My earnest prayer is that we may all qualify to practice this religion.

1. Bhagavad-Gita, 7:16
2. John 4:24
3. Ibid., 4:23-24
4. Ibid., 3:8
5. Ibid., 8:32
6. Matthew 5:8
7. Bhagavad-Gita, 3:27